Restaurant

By Jennifer Colby

21st Century Junior Library

Published in the United States of America by
Cherry Lake Publishing
Ann Arbor, Michigan
www.cherrylakepublishing.com

Content Adviser: Darcie Humphrey-Phillips owns and operates restaurants in Michigan.
Reading Adviser: Marla Conn MS, Ed., Literacy specialist, Read-Ability, Inc.

Photo Credits: © naka-stockphoto/Shutterstock Images, cover, 1; © Michael Shake/Shutterstock Images, 4; © Monkey Business Images/Shutterstock Images, 6; © andresr/iStock Images, 8; © goodluz/Shutterstock Images, 10; © oceanfishing/Shutterstock Images, 12; © Alinute Silzeviciute/Shutterstock Images, 14; © Mila Supinskaya/Shutterstock Images, 16; © Pressmaster/Shutterstock Images, 18; © Marcel Mooij/Shutterstock Images, 20

Library of Congress Cataloging-in-Publication Data
Names: Colby, Jennifer, 1971- author.
Title: Restaurant / by Jennifer Colby.
Description: Ann Arbor : Cherry Lake Publishing, [2016] | Series: 21st century junior library. Explore a workplace | Audience: K to grade 3. | Includes bibliographical references and index.
Identifiers: LCCN 2015047473| ISBN 9781634710770 (hardcover) | ISBN 9781634712750 (pbk.) | ISBN 9781634711760 (pdf) | ISBN 9781634713740 (ebook)
Subjects: LCSH: Restaurants–Juvenile literature. | Restaurants–Employees–Juvenile literature. | Food service–Vocational guidance–Juvenile literature.
Classification: LCC TX945 .C574 2016 | DDC 647.95/023–dc23
LC record available at http://lccn.loc.gov/2015047473

Cherry Lake Publishing would like to acknowledge the work of The Partnership for 21st Century Learning. Please visit *www.p21.org* for more information.

Printed in the United States of America
Corporate Graphics

CONTENTS

There are many kinds of restaurants.

What Is a Restaurant?

It is a fun night. Your family is eating out. You are at a **restaurant**. Can you smell the pizza? The **waiter**, or server, is carrying your pizza to your table. You are hungry! It is time to eat!

Some restaurants serve breakfast, lunch, and dinner.

Have you ever eaten at a restaurant? People go there to eat a meal. It takes many people to make a restaurant work. Would you like to work at one? Let's take a look at some restaurant jobs and find out.

Make a Guess!

What is a popular restaurant in your town? Write down your guess. Then ask 10 friends to name their favorite restaurant. Write down the results. Count the votes for each restaurant. Which one is the most popular? Was your guess correct?

The host takes you to your table.

Restaurant Workers

The first worker you meet is the **host**, or greeter. The host greets you when you walk in the door. Where would you like to sit? Do you want a seat by the window? Just tell the host. The host will try to find the best table for you. You might have to wait a bit, though.

Many cooks work in a kitchen. The chef is in charge of all the cooks.

A waiter comes to your table and wants to take your order. Look at the **menu**. What would you like to eat? The waiter will tell the workers in the kitchen. They will cook the meal you order.

The head **chef**, or kitchen manager, is in charge of the kitchen. The head chef tells the other chefs, cooks, or kitchen workers what to do. The chef also helps to decide what meals go on the menu.

A busser takes away your dishes when you are finished.

Waiters cannot do their jobs alone. **Bussers**, or service assistants, set the table before you arrive. They clear the dishes when you are done. The dishes go to the kitchen for a **dishwasher** to clean. Bussers and dishwashers make dining out more fun. Why? You do not have to clean up when you are done!

The menu shows all the items you
can choose from at a restaurant.

A **manager** runs the restaurant. Managers have many jobs. They hire the workers and plan the menu with the chef. They order and pay for restaurant supplies. They make the work schedule and pay the workers.

Managers must listen to what **customers** have to say. They want to make you happy. They want your family to come back again!

An inspector checks a restaurant kitchen.

An **inspector** makes sure the restaurant is clean and safe. Inspectors watch how workers handle food. Do they wash their hands often? Everything must be done right to pass inspection. The restaurant must make the changes the inspector tells it to.

Think!

There are many different kinds of restaurants, including school **cafeterias**. What makes a cafeteria different from other restaurants? Hint: Who carries your food to your table at school? Who clears your place when you are done? You do! A cafeteria has no host, waiters, or bussers.

Do you like to help cook meals at home?

Do You Want to Work at a Restaurant?

It is not too early to start planning ahead! Many people enjoy working at restaurants. Talk to workers when you go out to eat. What do they like best? Ask yourself questions. Do you like people? Do you like planning meals? Do you like cooking? Ask the adults in your family if you can help plan and cook meals.

Many famous chefs began their restaurant careers as dishwashers, maybe you will too!

A restaurant is a great place to work. You can get ready for a job in a restaurant by helping out at home. You can offer to set and clear your family's dinner table. Offering to help wash the dishes is also great practice. You can even help plan and cook your family's meals. Learn as much as you can now. Then you can decide if working at a restaurant is right for you!

Create!

Pretend your family's house is a restaurant. Give your restaurant a name. Create a menu. Show your family to the table. Give them the menu. Have them order a meal. Have an adult help you prepare and serve the meal. Congratulations! You just practiced the skills needed for many restaurant jobs.

GLOSSARY

bussers (BUHS-uhrz) workers who help waiters by setting and clearing tables

cafeterias (kaf-uh-TEER-ee-uh) restaurants where people get their own food and bring it back to their tables

chef (SHEF) a skilled cook who is often in charge of other cooks in a kitchen

customers (KUHS-tuh-murz) people who visit a business, such as a restaurant, to buy something or use a service

dishwasher (DISH-wah-shur) a person whose job is to wash dishes

host (HOHST) a person who greets people at a restaurant and shows them to their tables

inspector (in-SPEK-tuhr) a worker who checks restaurants to make sure they are safe and clean

manager (MAN-uh-jur) someone who is usually in charge of all the other workers

menu (MEN-yoo) a list of all the foods that can be ordered in a restaurant

restaurant (RES-tuh-rahnt) a place where people pay to eat meals prepared by other people

waiter (WAY-tur) someone who serves people food and drinks in a restaurant

FIND OUT MORE

BOOKS

Afromsky, Ryan. *I Have a Restaurant*. Del Mar, CA: Bettie Youngs Books, 2011.

Mason, Helen. *Chef*. New York: Gareth Stevens Publishing, 2014.

WEB SITES

Kids.gov—White House Chef
https://kids.usa.gov/watch-videos/jobs/white-house-chef/index.shtml
Learn about being the head chef at the White House.

TeensHealth—Eating Well While Eating Out
http://kidshealth.org/teen/food_fitness/nutrition/eating_out.html
Learn how to make healthy choices while eating out.

INDEX

ABOUT THE AUTHOR

Jennifer Colby is the author of many books for children. During high school, she was a dishwasher in a restaurant. Now she is a high school librarian in Michigan. She loves going out to eat so she does not have to wash the dishes.